DEDICATION

To my husband for always
supporting my magical moods!

My Magical Moods
The Magic of Me Series

www.authorbcummings.com

ISBN: 978-1-951597-32-0 (hardcover)
ISBN: 978-1-951597-33-7 (ebook)

Library of Congress Control Number: 2022902297

Illustrations by Nejla Shojaie
Book design by Nejla Shojaie, Maskrtáren and Dani Lurie
Editing by Laura Boffa, Tamara Rittershaus, Sam Pendleton

Printed in the USA
Signature Book Printing

First printing edition 2022.

Free Kids Press

MY MAGICAL MOODS

WRITTEN BY

BECKY CUMMINGS

ILLUSTRATED BY

NEJLA SHOJAIE

Like a seesaw up and down,
your mood can go from smile to frown.
Remember when you're feeling low,
up's the only way to go!

Listen closely to this life advice,
to lift your mood and feel nice!
Your joy and calm come from inside,
so up or down, enjoy the ride.

I CAN BE MUSICAL.

Turn on music, sing, or dance,
reggae, country, jazz, or trance.
Grab a flute, guitar, or drum.
Beatbox loud or softly hum.

I CAN BE OUTSIDE.

Sunshine kisses flood your face.

Barefoot toes prepare to race.

Birds and bugs will sing from trees.

Breathe in deep a fresh, cool breeze.

I CAN BE ACTIVE.

Walk or run, play sports, or bike,

get in nature, take a hike.

Pushups, planks, or jumping rope,

exercise will help you cope.

I CAN BE CREATIVE.

Paint or draw to feel the flow,

let imagination grow.

Use your hands to build or bake,

model cars or play dough cake.

I CAN SLEEP.

Warm and snuggled, wrapped in bed,

rest your body, rest your head.

Close your eyes and count some sheep.

Filled with peace, you go to sleep.

I CAN BE ALONE.

Quiet time is what you need:

journal writing, books to read.

Time to think and still your mind.

Calming down lets you unwind.

I CAN BE REFRESHED.

Slip on in a filled-up tub.

Make some bubbles, scrub-a-dub.

Take a shower, feel the heat,

water soothing hair to feet.

I CAN BE WITH ANIMALS.

Make friends with feathers, scales, or fur.

A bunny's kiss, a kitty's purr,

calms the heart and stops the tears.

Hello peace and good-bye fears.

I CAN BE SOCIAL.

Time with friends to laugh and play,

can bring you joy, improve your day.

A single tribe, we come from one,

brothers, sisters, having fun.

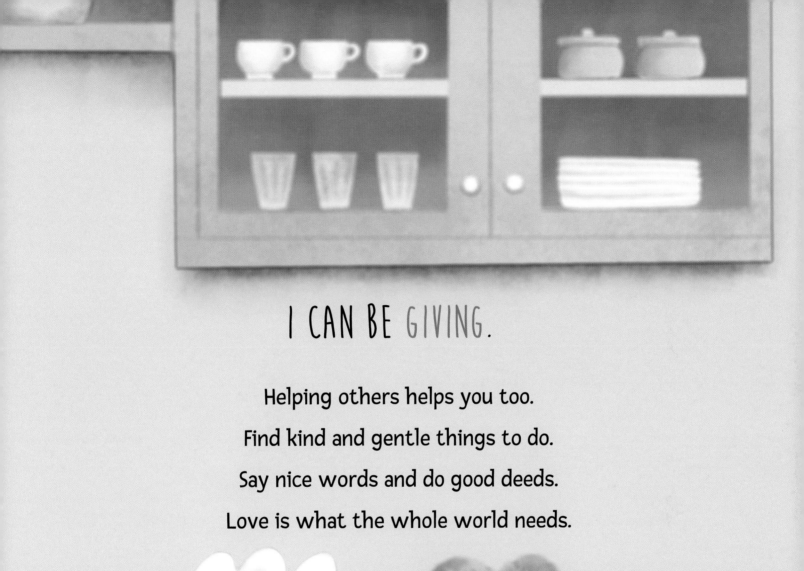

I CAN BE GIVING.

Helping others helps you too.

Find kind and gentle things to do.

Say nice words and do good deeds.

Love is what the whole world needs.

I CAN BE HEALTHY.

Did you know what you eat and drink

affects your body, how you think?

Luckily, Earth is quite the store.

Choose water, plants, and fruits galore!

I CAN BE PRESENT.

Pause and breathe in long and slow.
Connect yourself to Earth below.
Touch your heart and feel the beat,
sending peace from head to feet.

Teach yourself to change your mood.

You can adjust your attitude!

Lift your spirits and shine today.

Let your magic lead the way!

SPECIAL AS CAN BE,
THIS IS
THE MAGIC OF ME!

TIPS FOR HELPING CHILDREN LIFT THEIR MOODS

1. Model the strategies in the book when you are in a low mood. Label for children what you are doing and why. When they see you apply techniques to lift your spirits, they will try to use them as well.

2. When your child is in a low mood, refer back to this book and ask them to choose a technique to try. Use the symbols on the opposite page as a reminder of the 12 strategies discussed in this book. Feel free to make copies of the symbol page to serve as a tool to keep around the home or classroom.

3. At the end of the day, choose a time like dinner or bedtime to help your child reflect on their day. Ask them to share a moment when they had a low mood. Discuss it with them and ask them to share if they used a strategy to lift their mood. If they didn't, ask them what strategy they could have used to help.

ENJOY MORE BOOKS IN THIS SERIES BY BECKY CUMMINGS!

The Magic of Me
MY MAGICAL WORDS
WRITTEN BY Becky Cummings
ILLUSTRATED BY Zuzana Svobodová

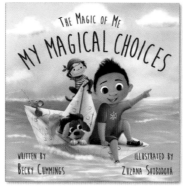

The Magic of Me
MY MAGICAL CHOICES
WRITTEN BY Becky Cummings
ILLUSTRATED BY Zuzana Svobodová

The Magic of Me
MY MAGICAL DREAMS
WRITTEN BY Becky Cummings
ILLUSTRATED BY Zuzana Svobodová

The Magic of Me
MY MAGICAL GIFTS
WRITTEN BY Becky Cummings
ILLUSTRATED BY Zuzana Svobodová

BECKY CUMMINGS

The MAGIC of ME
A KID'S GUIDE TO CREATING HAPPINESS

for older readers 8-12

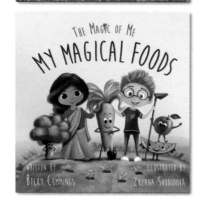

The Magic of Me
MY MAGICAL FOODS
WRITTEN BY Becky Cummings
ILLUSTRATED BY Zuzana Svobodová

The Magic of Me
MY MAGICAL FEELINGS
WRITTEN BY Becky Cummings
ILLUSTRATED BY Nejla Shojaie

www.authorbcummings.com